A Practical Guide

of Piping and Decorating
Special Designs for
Bride, Birthday, Christmas, Simnels
Easter and Presentation Cakes

Copyright © 2011 Read Books Ltd.
This book is copyright and may not be
reproduced or copied in any way without
the express permission of the publisher in writing

British Library Cataloguing-in-Publication Data
A catalogue record for this book is available from
the British Library

CONTENTS

Introductory 2

Cake Icing and Ornamentation 3

Utencils 6

Elementary Excercises 9

Writing in Sugar 14

Cake Coating with Royal Icing 18

Dividing-Out Rings 22

Simple Cake Top Designs 26

The Art of Stenciling 38

Marzipan Fruits and Flowers 49

How to Make your own Piped Flowers and Roses 60

The *Vintage Cookery Books* Series

A Short History of the Cook Book

One might be forgiven for thinking, in our age of celebrity chefs and glossy publications, that cook books are a relatively modern occurrence. However cook books have an incredibly long history, dating as far back as the first century CE.

The oldest collection of recipes that has survived in Europe is *De Re Coquinaria*, written in Latin. An early version was first compiled sometime in the first century and has often been attributed to the Roman gourmet, Marcus Gavius Apicius. An even earlier example (though less recognisable as a modern cook book), was also found in the Roman empire. This was the first known food writer – a Greek Sicilian named Archestratus, who lived in the fourth century BCE. He wrote a poem that spoke of using 'top quality and seasonal' ingredients, and insisted that flavours should not be masked by spices, herbs or other seasonings. Archestratus placed special importance on the simple preparation of fish.

Simplicity was abandoned and replaced by a culture of gastronomy as the Roman Empire developed however. By the time *De Re Coquinaria* was published, it contained 470 recipes calling for heavy use of spices and herbs. After a long interval, the first recipe books to be compiled in Europe since Late Antiquity started to appear in the thirteenth century. About a hundred are known to have survived, some fragmentary, from the age before printing. The earliest genuinely medieval recipes have been found in a Danish manuscript dating from around

1300, which in turn is a copy of older texts that date back to the early thirteenth century or perhaps earlier. Chinese cook books have also been found, dating to around this time – and one of the earliest surviving Chinese-language cookbooks; Hu Sihui's *Important Principles of Food and Drink* is believed to have been written in 1330.

German manuscripts are among the most numerous examples of cook books, among them being *The Book of Good Food* written in 1350 and *Kitchen Mastery* written in 1485. Two French collections are probably the most famous: *Le Viandier* ('The Provisioner') which was compiled in the late fourteenth century by Guillaume Tirel, and *The Householder of Paris*; a household book written by an anonymous middle class Parisian in the 1390s. Recipes originating in England include the earliest recorded recipe for ravioli, and the renowned *Forme of Cury* (mid-fourteenth century), compiled by the Master Cooks of King Richard II of England.

Cookbooks that serve as basic kitchen references (sometimes known as 'kitchen bibles') began to appear in the early modern period. They provided not just recipes but overall instructions for both kitchen technique and household management. Such books were written primarily for housewives and occasionally domestic servants, as opposed to professional cooks. Containing a veritable wealth of information, books such as *The Joy of Cooking* (USA), *La Bonne Cuisine de Madame E. Saint-Ange* (France), *The Art of Cookery* (UK), *Il Cucchiaio D'Argento* (Italy), and *A Gift to Young Housewives* (Russia) have served as records for entire national cuisines. With the advent of the printing press in the sixteenth and seventeenth centuries, numerous books were written on how to manage households and prepare food. In Holland and England especially, competition grew between the noble families as to who could prepare the most lavish banquet.

By the 1660s, cookery had progressed to an art form and good cooks were in demand. Many of these professional chefs took full advantage of the new trend, and published their own books detailing their recipes in competition with their rivals. By the nineteenth century, the Victorian preoccupation for domestic respectability brought about the emergence of cookery writing in its modern form. Although eclipsed in fame and regard by Isabella Beeton, the first modern cookery writer and compiler of recipes for the home was Eliza Acton. Her pioneering cookbook, *Modern Cookery for Private Families* (published in 1845), was aimed at the domestic reader rather than the professional cook or chef. This was an immensely influential book, and it established the format for modern writing about cookery.

The publication of *Modern Cookery* introduced the now-universal practice of listing the ingredients and suggested cooking times with each recipe. It also included the first recipe for Brussels sprouts. The book long survived its author, remaining in print until 1914 – functioning as an important influence on Isabella Beeton. Beeton went on to write and publish *Mrs Beeton's Book of Household Management* in twenty-four monthly parts between 1857 and 1861. Of the 1,112 pages detailing domestic issues, over 900 contained recipes, such that another popular name for the volume is *Mrs Beeton's Cookbook*. Most of the recipes were illustrated with coloured engravings, and it was the first book to show recipes in a format that is still used today. In 1896, the American cook Fannie Farmer published her illustrious work, *The Boston Cooking School Cookbook*, which contained some 1,849 recipes.

A good store of vintage cook books should be a kitchen staple for any creative cook. And as such, this series provides a collection of works, designed to instruct, inform and entertain the modern-day reader on times, peoples and foods of the past.

Today, the simple pleasures of practical household skills (so wonderfully demonstrated in these books) have been all but forgotten. Now, it's time to get back to basics. This series will take the reader back to the golden age of practical skills; an age where making and mending, cooking and preserving, brewing and bottling, were all done within the home.

The *Vintage Cookery Books* series hopes to bring old wisdom and classic techniques back to life, as we have so much to learn from 'the old ways' of cooking. Not only can these books provide a fascinating window into past societies, cultures and every-day life, but they also let us actively delve into our own history – with a taste of what, how and when, people ate, drank, and socialised. Enjoy.

Introductory.

The great success and cordial receptions which have attended the many thousands of copies of my various books on Cake Making, Icing Designs, etc., along with my many years' wide experience as teacher to the various schools, has enabled me to know the real wants of those commencing to study the art of Icing and Decorating, and to start them right at the beginning—from the mixing of the sugar to the finishing off by easy stages, of the complete Bride Cake.

It is with that sole object in mind that I have compiled this valuable book on Easy Icing Designs, explaining all in very simple language so that readers will have no trouble in following out my methods and instructions.

One glance through its pages and you see the numerous photo. plates—taken from actual work—which is sufficient to let one see that the price charged for this collection of popular designs is exceptionally low compared with other trade books.

This low price has been made possible by reason of the fact that large quantities of " Icing Made Easy " have been printed, and the least I can hope readers to do—if they are pleased with the publication—is kindly to recommend it to their friends.

Yours faithfully,
GEORGE F. BURTON,
Gold Medallist.

PARK ROAD,
BLACKPOOL.   . Tel. 1366.

Cake Icing and Ornamentation.

ICING.

A common difficulty which often confronts the average piper is in the selection of a suitable and appropriate design which, while conforming to requirements, combines neatness and pleasing effect with simplicity. For, be it noted, that simplicity of design, not elaborate, over-decorated effort, usually merits highest favour. In cake decoration, therefore, let this be a guiding principle.

Time-saving methods are very essential, therefore whatever means are adopted to this end are especially valuable particularly at festive seasons when exceptional demands are made. These conditions have to be met and successfully overcome.

In the course of my varied and extensive experience, gleaned in many high-class businesses, I have gained knowledge of the best and most effective systems whereby cakes may be decorated and embellished in the shortest available time, combined with a minimum of labour. In this direction readers will grasp the real practical value of my book. My designs are carefully thought out and selected specifically to meet the requirements of all pipers who desire to amplify and increase their variety of designs, changing this or that style as desired, obtaining new effects and combinations, yet retaining the indispensable time-economising methods throughout. If my instructions are carefully followed, beautiful cake-decoration may be accomplished in a very short space of time.

PIPING & ORNAMENTATION.

The first and most important stage of piping and ornamentation is in the preparation of the sugar. It is at this all-important stage that many pipers fail, making the inexcusable mistake of not beating up the sugar sufficiently. One may often see cakes neatly piped and decorated, yet the whole work is completely spoiled by the bad colour of the sugar. A common mistake is made in using too much blue ; in other cases insufficient is added.

My Method of Mixing Icing.

Be sure the utensils used are free from grease and dirt. A wood spattle must be used in preference to an iron spoon, as the latter is apt to be rusty. Fresh whites of eggs give the best results for cakes standing any length of time, and if compounds be used add one more drop of acid. Place the required quantity of whites of eggs in a large basin, gradually beat in a little sugar until the mixture is fairly stiff, then add sufficient blue to bring out a blue tint (ultramarine blue dissolved in a little boiling water gives the most satisfactory results). Add three drops of acetic acid to each medium-sized egg "white," continue to beat the icing briskly for fully a quarter-of-an-hour, and remember not to add the sugar rapidly or the mixture will become heavy and difficult to manipulate. The object of the continuous brisk beating with the spattle is to obtain a clear, light, pliable icing, duly incorporated with air. When finished the icing must always be covered with a perfectly clean damp cloth.

The Piping Bag.

Now to proceed with the making of the paper bag. This bag, I may add, is much handier to use than a syringe. It is advisable to use the finest parchment paper (for size see page 6). Take hold of the cut paper in your left hand the same way as it is illustrated, your left thumb placed on the upper part of the long side, the centre point towards you. With your right-hand turn the first point inward, the left thumb forming the point of the bag. Fold over until the left point of the triangle is reached, then fasten the top of your completed bag with this point. Cut off three-quarters of an inch from the bottom to allow the point of your tube to pass half-way through. Then half fill the bag with icing, securely fastening the top.

ICING TUBES.

No.	Name	No.	Name	No.	Name	No.	Name
1	PLAIN	2	PLAIN	3	PLAIN	4	Small Border
5	ROPE	6	FINE SIX STAR	7	LARGE SIX STAR	8	EIGHT STAR
9	FANCY BAND	10	LARGE LEAF	11	ROSE	12	SHELL
13	FIVE STAR	14	TEN STAR	15	DAHLIA	16	Double Thread
17	SMALL LEAF	18	BENT ROSE	19	FOUR STAR	20	FINE ROPE
21	TWELVE STAR	22	BORDER	23	HOLLOW BAND	24	RIBBON
25	SIDE BAND	26	GRAPE	27	FANCY STAR	28	Forget-me-Not
29	Plain Band	30	Small Plain Band	31	CLEMATIS	32	THREE THREAD
33	SCROLL	34	MIDDLE BAND	35	SMALL BAND	36	BENT ROSE
37	FANCY BAND	38	HOLLOW BAND	39	FANCY RIBBON	40	CENTRE BAND
41	TULIP	42	SMALL ROSE				

ICING TUBES FOR USE WITH PAPER BAGS.

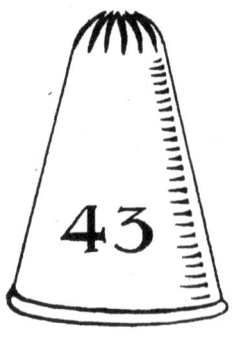

BISCUIT TUBES No. 43 and 44. Used generally with the Savoy Bags.

Icing made easy

Utensils

As illustrated on page 7.

No. 1—Fine Parchment Paper for Icing Bag. Size 10ins. by 12ins. by 15ins.

No. 2—Icing Bag fitted with Tube ready for filling with sugar.

No. 3—Icing Tubes for Paper Bag use.

No. 4—Patent Dividing Rings (full particulars given on pages 22 and 23).

No. 5—Showing cake top divided into eight equal parts.

No. 6—Set of Compasses.

No. 7—Icing Knives.

No. 8—Wood Revolving Stand.

No. 9—Dummy used for practice work.

ICING SYRINGE.

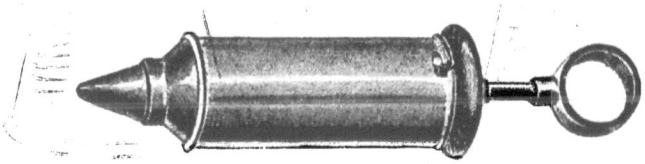

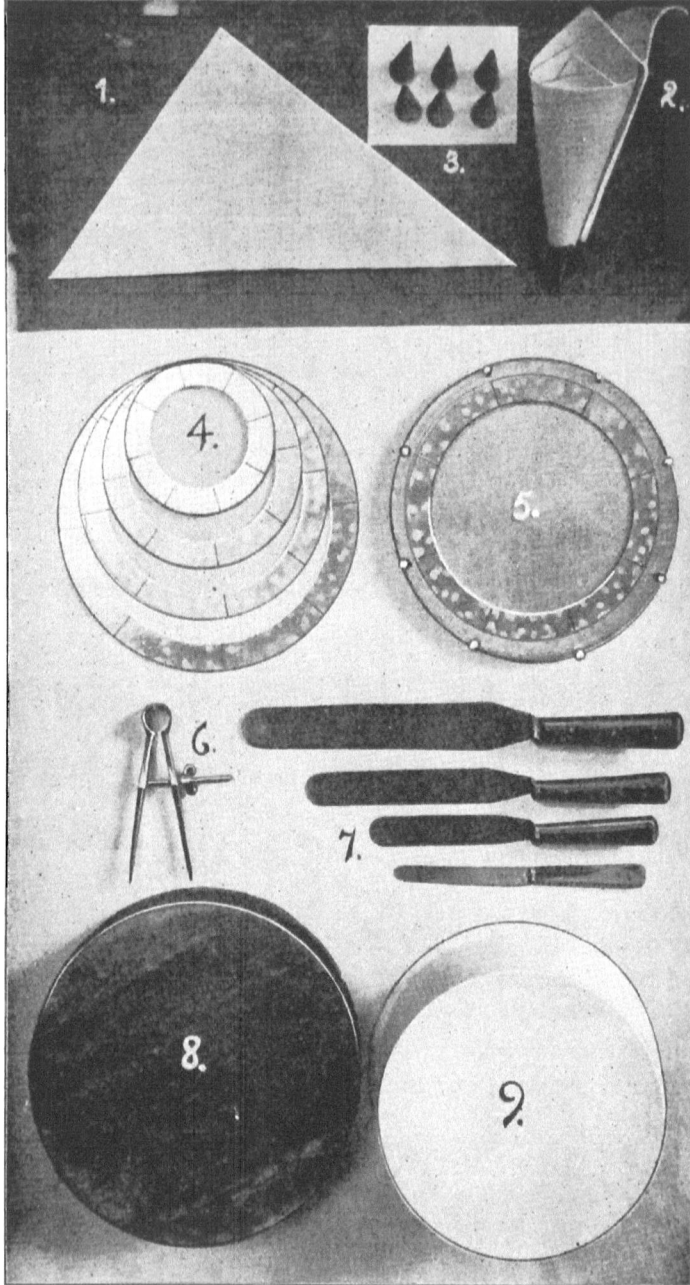

How to Hold Your Tube and Bag.

There is always a right and wrong way in handling the Icing Bags. You will notice that every tube that you use—whatever metal it is made from—has a seam. That is where the tube is joined and soldered together. If you will run your finger round the inside of any tube you will soon find out where the joining is, and when icing sugar is pressed through a tube it will drag on the seam side, Therefore always see that the seam of your tube is nearest to the cake when using. Now to hold the bag. Always keep your right thumb at the back of the bag, your first finger down the side and rest the bag on your second finger and keep your third and fourth fingers closed, just as if you were holding a pen. Do not grasp clumsily—quite easily and freely. Don't try to pipe by holding the bag with your two hands. This is a big mistake that is often done. Your left hand is needed to rest your right hand on, and is a very valuable help in keeping your lines steady, and care should also be taken when resting your right hand on your left to see that you do not press too firmly. You must be able to move your bag round easily and quickly. Always wipe your tube end with a damp cloth to avoid any hard sugar accumulating at the end of the tube. After mastering the making of the sugar and the paper bag, which is very important if you are to make a success in piping, we will now proceed with the first exercises (Plate A).

Elementary Exercises.

PLATE A.

The above exercises will be found of great value in commencing to pipe, and I would advise you to try them several times over on a tin or piece of glass with plain tube No. 2, taking the icing off before it sets and using it again and again. Keep the tube just running along the tin. No doubt you will produce some very fantastic examples at first, which may dismay you. Some pupils appear to lose heart by not obtaining correct results in their first efforts. Do not be disheartened by a trifling non-success. Remember improvement comes from thoughtful and repeated practice.

Elementary Exercises.

PLATE B.
CRINKLE LINES. NO. 2 TUBE.

The above plate, sketched out as Plate A, using the same tube, No. 2, this being termed in piping phraseology a "crinkled" line. This gives a showy effect as compared with the plain line, and is very often used for bottom and side borders. In piping towards you twist the icing to the left, and in making lines in the contrary direction, namely, from you, twist to the right, as marked up and down. A nice, regular, even twist is desired. In the last four examples pipe the centre wider and taper off at the ends.

Elementary Exercises.

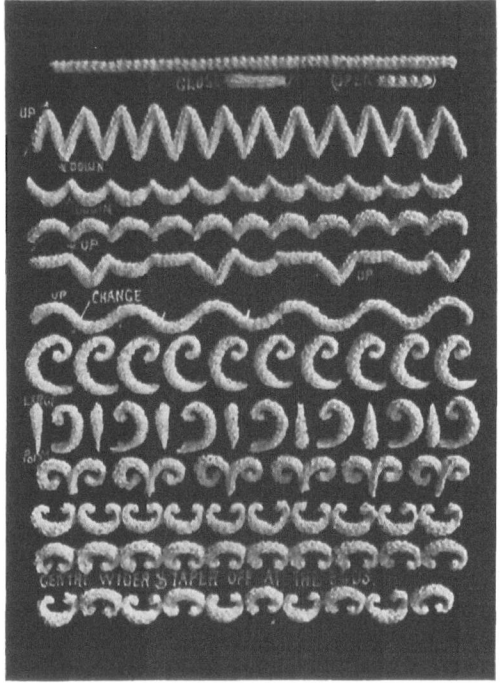

PLATE C.

CRINKLE LINES. NO. 5 STAR TUBE.

Follow out the same directions as Plate B, but change the plain tube for a small star tube, carefully noting all previous instructions. If these designs be not carefully done, if lapped too close, the designs run in a mingled mass; if too open an irregular line is formed. Various sizes of star tubes can be used for the above crinkled lines, using the larger tube for a bolder border. Try keeping your curves all the same size.

PLATE D.

BUILDING UP THE DESIGN.

Trace over the crinkled line (made with the star tube) with the plain tube No. 3, then allow the work to set a little. Then trace over this No. 3 line with the finer plain tube No. 2, taking care to keep all lines plumb and true to sketch. Tone down or reduce any points. To complete, again trace over with the finest plain tube, keeping the curves symmetrical and free from corners.

After mastering the exercises given you will have trained your hand and eye to space out proportionately the outer line, which must run correctly and quite true to the first line, keeping parallel lines at equal distances until completed ; remember that parallel lines never meet but are the same distance apart. Also remember that improvement assuredly comes from persistent effort and continued practice. Give your mind to your task and proficiency will readily be won.

These preliminaries being properly completed, the first stages of ornamentation may now be commenced.

First exercises in piping may be compared to the learning of shorthand : once the letters are mastered complete words may easily be written.

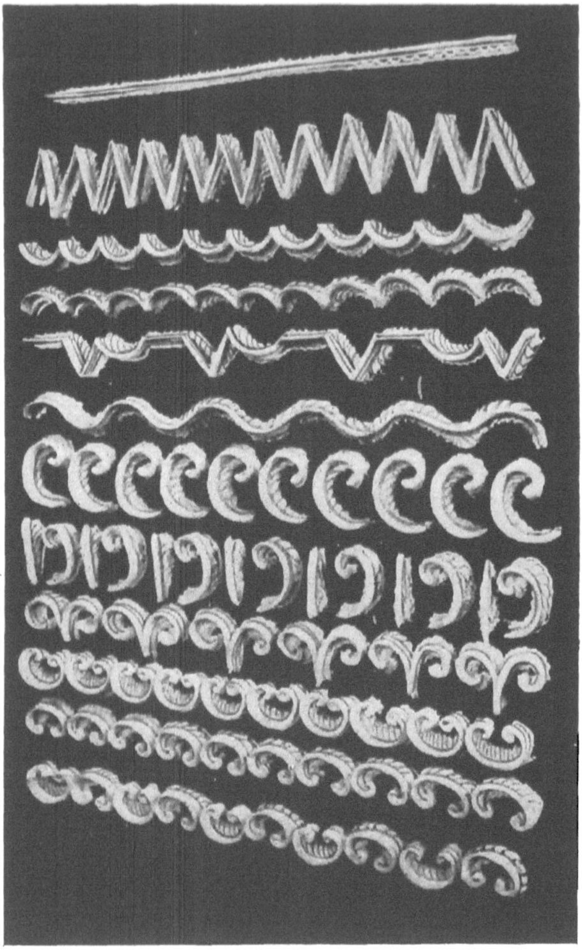

PLATE D.   EXERCISES (Final Plate of Previous Exercises).

Writing in Sugar

This work is very important, and, when skill is acquired, is most useful. The following cakes are always suitable for inscriptions :—Golden and Silver Wedding, Birthday, Simnel, Christmas, and other Celebration Cakes. Writing takes up less time and fills up the cake-surface quicker than elaborate ornamentation ; in addition, it is always pleasing and acceptable when neatly and tastefully executed. Writing, to look really well, must be adequately built up, resembling letters carved out of the solid piece or as usually termed " block letters." Do not be afraid, therefore, of building up boldly, exactly as in Plate D, page 13.

PLATE E.

No. 1.—When commencing writing in sugar it is always advisable to sketch out your inscription or motto first with the finest plain tube ; this is essential to enable you to obtain true uniformity. Note carefully always to draft the first portions of the letters B.F.E.H.I.L.M.N. perfectly straight, and always cross the letter T on the slant to equalise the space as with other letters.

No. 2.—Trace over the sketched line with plain tube No. 3. Special care must be taken at this point to make all the letters of equal size, also in forming the letters E.F.R.Y. to show no blobs on completion. In the perfect letter one fails to see the joints and a regular even surface is obtained.

No. 3.—As soon as the work is set, again trace over with the plain tube No. 2, keeping exactly on the lines piped out by No. 3. At this stage guard against enlarging on the first or original lines, or even making them smaller ; either error will spoil the imprint. Keep a bold, firm line, exactly in the centre.

How to Write with Sugar.

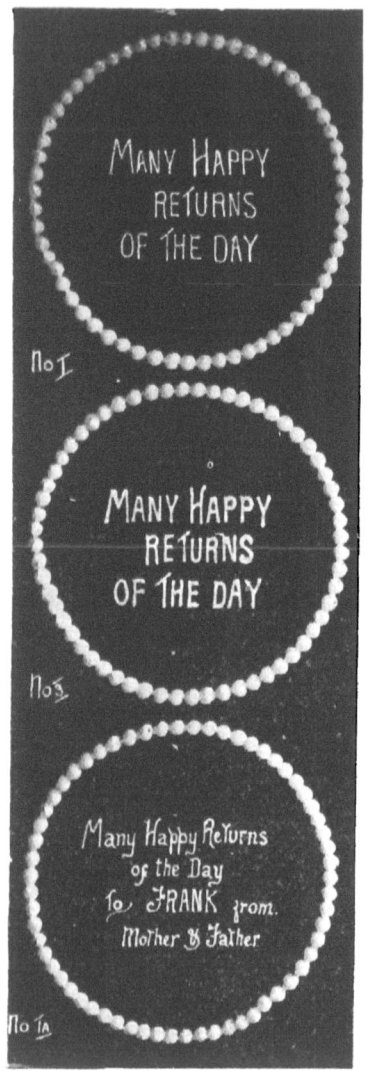

PLATE E.

Writing in Sugar—*(continued)*

No. 4.—Now for the final, the last but most important line of the series. This is added when the previous line has set, the finest plain tube being used for the purpose. This brings the inscription to a fine and delicate finish. For Christmas and Birthday Cakes it is usual to finish off with coloured sugar.

Nos. 1a and 2a.—Follow the previous instructions, omitting the capital letters and generally writing finer and smaller, as a large motto can always be piped on a small cake. This writing is very adaptable for chocolate medallions, network piping, and relief piping.

If the foregoing instructions are carefully observed, I feel confident that splendid results will be obtained.

Plate F.

This plate exhibits striking examples of the various uses to which writing may be devoted, and will probably be found an acceptable form for customers' special requirements in this direction.

Now let me impress upon you when first commencing writing to use good sugar. With that I mean well beaten up; and another very important feature is to keep your letters very close together—you cannot get the letters too close as long as they do not touch one another.

Birthday and Christmas Cakes can be finished off with delicate colours in rose pink, chocolate, green. Care should be taken not to get your colours too deep.

Suitable Writings for Parties and special occasions.

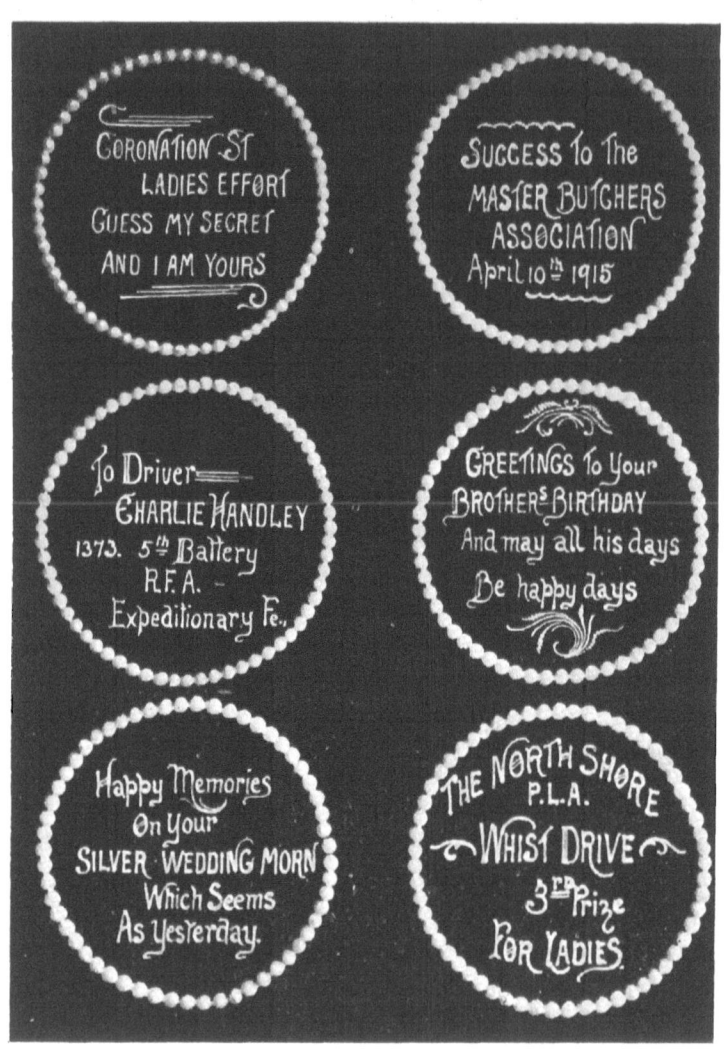

Plate F.

Cake Coating with Royal Icing

Cake Coating is very important in Cake Decorating, and to help you to get a smooth surface on the cakes I have included the three following illustrations :—

PLATE G (Page 19).

Cover the top of the cake first, keeping the point of your icing knife in the centre of the cake all the time you are turning the stand with your left hand. To finish off draw the knife gently to the edge. Please note to have the icing sugar just a little softer than for piping.

PLATE H (Page 20).

When you have finished the top of the cake, cover the sides all over roughly. Then hold your hand and knife in the same position as shown in illustration. Keep your first finger well down the blade of the knife, which helps to keep the knife steady.

PLATE I (Page 21).

This Plate shows the finish of the two previous Plates. After finishing off the sides as in Plate H, you will find a rough edge of icing left on where the top of the cake and the sides finish. Now by just letting your palette knife rest flat on the edge and turning the revolving stand round you can very easily take off all surplus sugar, taking about four inches off at one turn round. Then wipe the sugar off the knife and proceed until you have been all round the cake edge.

It is very essential to ice perfectly to use a revolving stand ; also a stiff palette knife.

Wedding Cakes require two coatings of sugar. First coat to settle the crumbs and to get a solid foundation. The second coat of icing to be added when the first is set quite hard to secure a more level and smooth surface.

Cake Top Coating

PLATE G.

Cake Side Coating

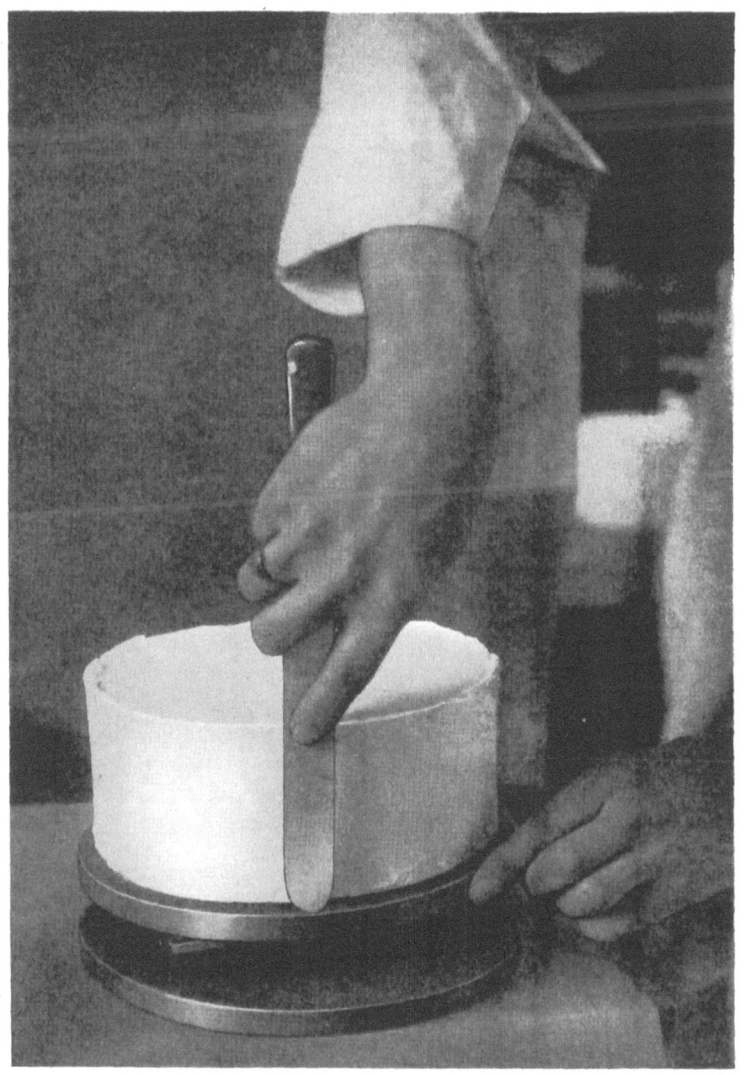

PLATE H.

Bride Cake Icing

PLATE I.

Dividing-Out Rings

(Patent No. 198245).

The keynote to the success of Cake Decorating is making perfectly sure that your divisions are quite true and accurate. Nothing looks worse than unbalanced designs.

You will find the Dividing-Out Rings a great help in your spacing out, and in securing a true centre; in addition, they will save you a tremendous amount of time.

One side of the Rings is marked out into eight equal divisions, and the other side is divided into six equal divisions.

Both sides can be used for marking out cakes. Simple to use and nothing to get out of order.

The Centre Disc will be found very useful for spacing names in centres of cakes as illustrated on Page 29.

Dividing-Out Rings

(Patent No. 198245).

The above illustration shows at a glance how quickly and easily you can divide your cakes into equal sections. Simply place the ring on the top of the cake and dot out with your piping bag. These Patent Dividing-Out Rings are now used by the leading bakers and confectioners throughout the present age. The rings are made up in sets so as to fit any size of cake, and are made of a strong material in order to last a lifetime.

A complete reference book for Bakers and Confectioners :: ::

"CAKE-MAKING ICING DESIGNS and BREAD"

Profusely Illustrated, including several Coloured Plates :: :: :: :: Yours

for **11/-** *post paid!*

Burton's Books are mines of information you cannot afford to miss :: Address

Geo. Burton :: Park Road
——————— BLACKPOOL ———————

Sketching Out Cake Top Designs.

Sketching out the design is a matter of first importance, requiring that all curves and lines shall be laid in correct geometrical form. We are bound, therefore, to divide the cake top into equal parts or sections. This is very quickly done by the aid of a Set of Rings, thus saving time in ruling and measuring. Place the rings of requisite size on the top of the cake, marking out with your icing bag the points you may require for guidance, as shown on page 23. On no account must a black or blue pencil be used. A sharp instrument is most useful for marking out. A pair of compasses will be found very useful in making measurements and marking out side and bottom borders. The cake now being divided into sections, we are quite ready to commence with the selected design, bearing in mind that it is not always the most decorated cake, nor the one with most work on, that looks the best, but more often the one with the neatest simple curves and true symmetrical lines.

Plate J.

For our first example we will take the first plate of my collection of Cake Tops, these comprising six simple yet effective designs. Divide out the cake into eight equal parts by the aid of the rings. Now commence to sketch out the copy pattern with the plain tube No. 2, completing the largest curves first. Care must be taken to make each part of equal distance from the other, the circular portions being nicely rounded off.

Plate K.

Shows the second stage of Plate J. With the star tube No. 5 crinkle the line exactly on the sketched line as on previous plate, running each curve neatly round and flowing into each other. When you have finished two curves stop and look back at the first one to see if you are getting them the same in size and detail.

Simple Cake Top Designs.

PLATE J.

Icing made easy

Simple Cake Top Designs.

PLATE K.

Simple Cake Top Designs.

SUITABLE FOR CHRISTMAS, BIRTHDAY AND SIMNELS.

PLATE L

is the finished Cake Top Designs of the two previous plates and you will at a glance see the difference from the last plate. When you have completed your design with the star tube and made a solid foundation, we then commence building up with plain tube No. 2. In building up you must remember to keep true to the curves or lines and keep the tube low down so that your icing is going just where you require it. You have a far better control over your icing sugar coming out of the tube when almost touching than when holding your tube high up in the air.

Build up your lines say four or six lines high. It is not wise to build up too quickly—see that one set of lines are almost dry before adding more, otherwise your curves will start swaying with the weight of the icing.

There is no fixed rule as to how high to build up your designs. This has to be guided by how much time you wish to spend on the cake. The higher you build up the nicer the design should look, provided you keep quite true to your outlay.

It is also advisable to vary your height of building up if you have two or more lines or curves running parallel to one another. Make your largest curve the highest and taper down to the centre of the cake.

Keep the lines or curves round the wording very fine and delicate by using the fine tube No. 1.

PLATE L.

Simple Cake Top Designs

SUITABLE FOR CHRISTMAS, BIRTHDAY AND SIMNELS.

1.—Divide into eight divisions. Simple half-curve design, keeping the parallel curved lines close together and drawn in at the ends. The ship in centre is outlined first with plain tube and run in after with soft icing.

2.—Divide into eight. A design somewhat like No. 1, being simple and suitable for Chocolate and Layer Cakes.

3.—Divide into sixteen by just doubling the eight-division ring. The main feature in this design is getting the " C " curves all the same size, afterwards draw in the smaller lines without showing any rough lines or points.

4.—Divide into eight, making use of the Dividing-Out Rings to secure getting the double circle. The centre scroll is suitable for greetings or mottoes.

5.—Divide into eight. First work out the square by the aid of a small ruler. You will be able to manage this design quite easily.

6.—Divide into eight. Quarter out the top first. Afterwards proceed, making the largest curves first, taking care to match one side with the other.

Simple Cake Top Designs

PLATE M.

Simple Cake Top Designs

SUITABLE FOR CHRISTMAS, BIRTHDAY AND SIMNELS.

1.—Divide into six divisions and scratch a treble triangle keeping the lines about one-eighth of an inch apart, the centre being worked from the small ring in Dividing-Out Set. In finishing the six scrolls round the edge of the cake, be careful to finish off all the lines on one point.

2.—Divide into six. This design is more for pupils to practice with the rings and compass to show what pleasing designs, can be obtained from circles.

3.—Divide into eight, then work the four circles two-thirds round. The parallel lines must be kept very close together, and also join the icing very clear at the points to give a fine finish.

4.—Divide into four. This is a design worked entirely from the compasses, the four large circles first, working in the smaller ones afterwards.

5.—Divide into six, only using one triangle as guide lines for the three circles, filling in the smaller lines and curves last.

6.—Divide into eight, using a double ring to work in the smaller part circles and finish off with very fine lines from No. 1 tube.

Icing made easy

Simple Cake Top Designs

Simple Cake Top Designs

SUITABLE FOR CHRISTMAS, BIRTHDAY AND SIMNELS.

1.—Twelve divisions, Sunflower design. Use the small circle from Dividing-Out Set to get the centre true. Finish off the points very fine. Star tube base for the larger curves.

2.—Twelve divisions. Scratch from point to point very fine and then work in the centre straight lines from the edge of the cake about half the distance to the centre. Afterwards work round the curves and finish off neatly in the centre.

3.—Six divisions, triangle design. Simply trace over your scratch line with your No. 2 plain tube. Fill in the curves with star tube No. 5, also the ends of triangle points.

4.—Twelve divisions, after the style of No. 3. A very effective design built up on the double " C " curves with plain tube. Care should be taken to keep the lines the same distance apart and very close together without touching each other.

5.—Twelve divisions. Showing what an attractive border the double " C " curve makes if kept all one uniform size. There is no reason why you should not adopt this design for your Wedding Cakes also.

6.—Twelve divisions as for No. 5 and the exact curves only the opposite way round. The centre, as in No. 5, can be filled in with flowers or any motto.

Simple Cake Top Designs

PLATE O.

Simple Cake Top Designs

SUITABLE FOR CHRISTMAS, BIRTHDAY AND SIMNELS.

1.—Divide out into four. Large curve design. Scratch from point to point, getting cross in centre. Build well up the inner curve and other two large curves that should run parallel.

2.—Eight divisions. Scratch from point to point and work into the divisions an even double " C " curve. Build up with plain tube, also add small dots.

3.—Sixteen divisions. Scratch lines very faint. Work centre into points and work the star tube lines in first.

4.—Four divisions. The cake top is worked as No. 1. Care should be taken in building up the lines.

5.—Eight divisions. The Owl design, which is suitable for a large cake top only. Be careful in finishing off the points at the centre.

6.—Four divisions. The Acorn design. This also is only suitable for large cakes and is more difficult on account of the centre curves, but looks quite well if the lines are kept true.

Icing made easy

Simple Cake Top Designs

PLATE P.

The Art of Stencilling

The art of stencil using is simplicity itself and is coming more to the front each year—you have only to glance at the trade papers from week to week to read what the leading experts and well-known lecturers say as to the value of stencils—thus providing a very profitable and commercial proposition for our trade, not only as a time-saver, but a great saver in sugar and other materials. These few illustrations and notes given will, I hope, be useful and helpful to you in obtaining the best results.

You require icing sugar to be well beaten up and just a shade stiffer than for piping. It is advisable if you have not tried stencilling previously to practice a few times on a flat tin before decorating cakes.

Be very particular to hold the stencil quite firm with the left hand, as a slight slip will completely spoil the whole design.

Do not, when spreading your icing over the stencils, allow the stencil to move.

Do not put too much sugar on stencil when spreading.

Do not overcrowd your designs.

Do not use the stencils before first dividing out your cake.

Always wipe the stencil after using.

Always use the arrow side upwards.

The Crank Palette Knife will be found the most suitable for stencilling.

Icing made easy

The Art of Stencilling—*continued*.

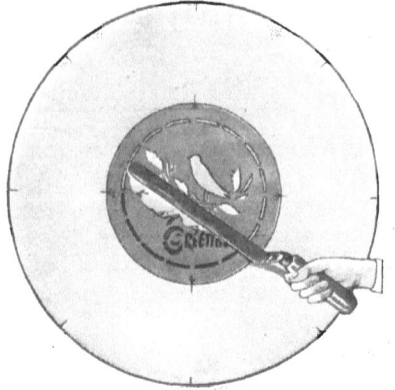

PLATE I. CAKE TOP.
INSTRUCTIONS.

Divide out your cake top into eight equal parts with the same size of dividing-out ring, as shown on page 23, just marking on the edge of the cake where the marks come.

Afterwards scratch (by the aid of ruler) a very faint line across the top of cake to bottom and from left to right. This will divide your cake into four equal parts.

Then place Stencil No. 51 so that the small arrows on four sides of the stencil are exactly on your dividing lines.

Keep a firm grip with left hand and spread over your Royal Icing with crank pallette.

PLATE II. CAKE TOP.
INSTRUCTIONS—*continued*.

Proceed exactly the same way with your Stencil No. 66, then No. 57. Be very particular that the small arrow on the stencil is exactly on your marked-out line each time you use any stencil. Care should also be taken not to use too much icing sugar at one operation.

PLATE III. CAKE TOP.

Finished example of the two previous Plates. Simple, neat and attractive, yet using very little sugar and finished off in a few seconds.

The Art of Stencilling—*continued*

PLATE IV. FINISHED CAKE TOP.

Use Stencils No. 51, 65, 74.

There is no end of scope in making up your own designs, but care should be taken not to overcrowd.

Our range of Stencils are specially assorted to fit any size of cake.

PLATE V. FINISHED CAKE TOP.

Use Stencils No. 50, 67, 75.

You may divide your cakes into as many divisions as you wish, and make quite attractive and tasteful borders by repeating the same stencil all round the cake.

PLATE VI. FINISHED CAKE TOP.

Use Stencils No. 49, 66, 75a.

Marshmallow and butter cream, also coloured jellies and chocolate can be used in the same way with the Stencils, which produces effective designs and decorations, enabling the maker to give good value in cheap sandwiches and layer cakes.

Christmas Cake Top Designs

Icing made easy

Christmas Cake Top Designs.

Icing made easy

BURTON'S STENCILS
ARE ALL
CUT FROM
STRONG METAL

Border Designs for Cake Sides.

STENCILS are the coming thing

If you have not commenced to use them, you should do so immediately

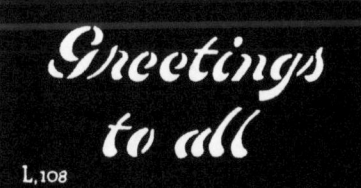

GEO. BURTON'S STENCILS
(CUT FROM STRONG METAL)
WILL BUILD UP YOUR TRADE.

Send for a Set of CAKE TOP MOTTOES !

Stencils for Cake Top Designs

Icing made easy

PLATE Q.

CAKE TOP DESIGNS FINISHED OFF WITH SMALL MARZIPAN FRUITS AND SILVER LEAVES.

Marzipan Fruits and Flowers

The following Mixing will be found very useful for both Marzipan Fruits and Flowers, and as both fruits and flowers can be introduced along with the icing, beautiful designs can be accomplished.

Mixing No. 1—MARZIPAN FOR SMALL FRUITS.
1 lb. Marzipan.
1 lb. Icing Sugar.

Method.—Work the above together to make into a nice moulding dough. Keep under a basin to avoid crust forming.

Mixing No. 2—MARZIPAN FOR ROSES AND FLOWERS.
1 lb. Marzipan.
1 lb. Icing Sugar.
¼ lb. Gum Paste.

Method.—Same as above.

GUM PASTE.

1 oz. Gum Tragacanth.
5 ozs. Water.
1¾ lbs. Best Icing Sugar (approx.)

Method.—Soak the Gum Tragacanth for 24 hours. Mix well, adding the sugar gradually (a little at a time) until mixed into a nice smooth pliable dough. A marble slab is very useful for working Gum Paste. Cover over with damp cloth to prevent crusting. Dust with cornflour and use as required.

This mixture is suitable for pinning out in various shapes, including placques for stencils or pressed into various moulds for birds and scrolls.

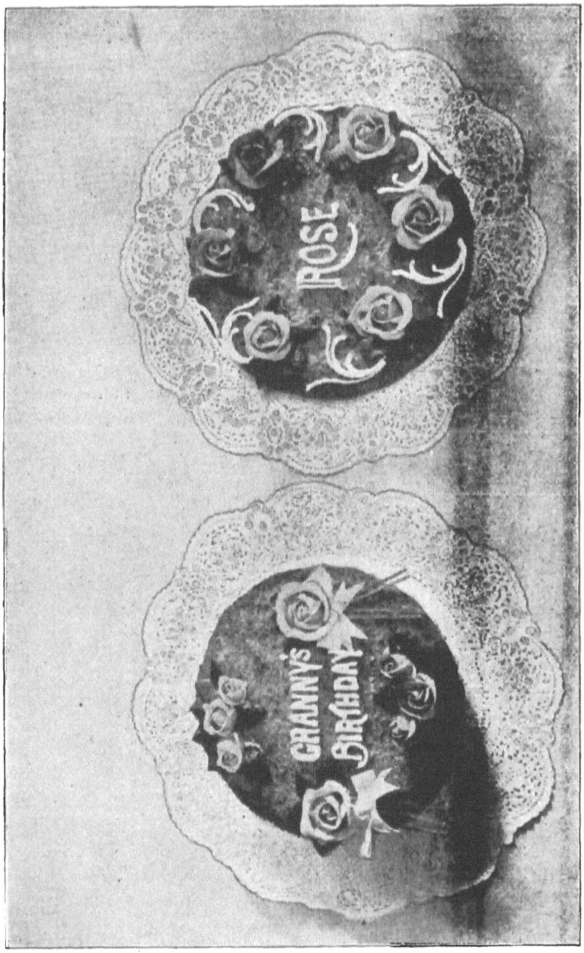

PLATE U.

ALMOND PASTE COVERED CAKES FINISHED OFF WITH MARZIPAN ROSES AND GREEN LEAVES.

Icing made easy

PLATE V.
ALMOND PASTE COVERED CAKES FINISHED OFF WITH CRYSTALISED VIOLETS AND ANGELICA.

Brides' Cakes.

6 lbs. Butter.
4 lbs. Brown Sugar.
1 lb. Castor Sugar.
5 lbs. Flour.
5 pints Eggs.
16 lbs. Currants.
5 lbs. Peel (mixed).
5 lbs. Sultanas.
2½ lbs. Citron Peel.
Zest of four Lemons.
6 ozs. Spice.
½ oz. Nutmeg.
1 oz. Salt.
1 lb. Chopped Almonds.
½ lb. Ground Almonds.
A little Essence Vanilla.

Simnel Cakes

3 lbs. Butter.
1 lb. 5 ozs. Compound Fat.
3 lbs. 15 ozs. Sugar.
4 lbs. 13 ozs. Flour.
3½ lbs. Sultanas.
12 lbs. Currants.
2 lbs. Peel.
2 ozs. Spice.
1 oz. Nutmeg.
1 lb. Ground Almonds.
2 quarts Eggs.
½ lb. Glycerine.
A little Black Jack or Choc. Colour to darken
Essence Lemon.

Method for above Mixings

Beat butter and sugar up fairly light. Add Black Jack to make a nice golden colour. Add eggs a few at a time. When all eggs have been beaten in add the flour, which should be sifted. Then add all other ingredients. Bake these cakes in cool oven—260 degs.

Icing made easy

PLATE W. SMALL BIRTHDAY CAKE.

Divide the cake top into eight parts, sketch out eight equal circles, then crinkle with star tube and build up the lines with graduating plain tubes. For the bottom border, use a large star tube and form shells from the bottom of the cake to the centre, finishing at a point. Then run the curves over the finish of the shells and see that all the ends of circles are finished smooth.

Mottoes may be written in any style or finish to suit clients' desires.

BRIDE CAKE IN EASY STAGES.
PLATE X.

Fig. 1 shows you how to divide your cake top and border into eight equal divisions and to line round ready for the network, No. 2 tube being used. The bottom curves are to be worked on the edge of the cake.

Fig. 2.—Trace over with Star tube No. 5, crinkled and tapered to the points. Add two extra lines in the centre and commence the three lines of network. The centre line should be on the edge of the cake.

Fig. 3.—Building up the Network. Network always looks nice if neatly done. Try to keep the squares all the same size. Fig. 3 shows various stages of adding lines. Keep the lines as close together as you can get them without touching and finish off the lines without any points or blobs of sugar.

Fig. 4.—Completed Wedding Cake Top. You will notice the network has been added to fill up and complete the border from side to side. The lines in the centre also built up in steps from the centre of the cake. A small rose and two silver leaves placed on each point improve the finish.

Figs. 5 and 6 are simple curves continued round the side of the cake to form a centre border. Sketch out as in Fig. 5. Afterwards build up and line round with plain tubes No. 1 and No. 2.

Fig. 7.—Bottom borders. These should always be brought out bold to match your top edge border. Divide your cake into eight equal parts then sketch out and bring out the bottom curve with Star tube No. 7. Line over with tube No. 2. Afterwards terrile from top to bottom, keeping the lines close together.

Fig. 8.—Finish off with plain tubes No. 2 and then No. 1. Take note that the finish curves should cover up the rough points of the terrile work and be joined neatly together at the points.

Bride Cake Ornamenting in stages

PLATE X.

Christmas Cakes

3½ lbs. Butter.
5½ lbs. Brown Sugar.
1½ lbs. Fat.
6 lbs. Flour.
11 lbs. Currants.
3½ lbs. Mixed Peel.
6 lbs. Sultanas.
1 lb. Split Almonds.
2 ozs. Spice.
¼ lb. Glycerine.
5 pints Eggs.
A little Black Jack.
Essence Lemon.

Birthday Cakes

1½ lbs. Butter.
½ lb. Compound Fat.
2¼ lbs. Sugar (Brown).
1 Quart Eggs.
3 lbs. Flour.
4 ozs. Cornflour.
½ oz. Powder.
1 lb. Citron Peel.
2 lbs. Currants.
2 lbs. Sultanas.
¼ oz. Nutmeg.
⅛ oz. Spice.
1 gill Milk.

Method for above Mixings.

Beat up butter and sugar fairly light. Add glycerine and Black Jack to make into a nice golden colour. Add eggs a few at a time. When all eggs are in, stir in flour, spice, nutmeg, and lastly add fruit and almonds. Bake these cakes in oven 260 deg.

Icing made easy

PLATE Y.
CHRISTMAS CAKE FINISHED OFF WITH HOLLOW NET NAILS AND SCROLLS.

ALMOND PASTE

Suitable for all kinds of cakes.

1 lb. Finest Ground Almonds.   1 lb. Castor Sugar.
2 Eggs.

Method.—Blend well together and mix to a firm paste with the eggs, adding a little lemon essence. It is an advantage before mixing with eggs to place the sugar and almonds in the oven and nicely warm them through. When rolling the paste with pin to thickness required dust the table with a little sugar to prevent sticking.

Damp the cake top over with egg before placing on the almond paste.

Decorated Birthday and Christmas Cakes Finished off in Colours.

PLATE Z.

PLATE AA.
THREE-TIER BRIDE CAKE.
HOLLOW NETS, NETWORK AND SCROLL BORDERS.

How to Make your own Piped Flowers and Roses.

In flower making be sure you have well beaten up sugar. If you use colourings add a little more dry sugar. Tubes used in flower making are very much the same, some being a little more curved than others. Tubes Nos. 11, 18, 36 and 42 on Page 5 are all you require for a variety.

Use the wide end of the tube always at the bottom of the nail, and practice the first petal as in the first line A, No. 1. The flowers are worked on this principle when you have mastered the first petal, which will require a little practice to get a fine edge on the outer side.

The centres of the daisies are piped round with plain tube No. 2, keeping the centre hollow and touching up with a little colour to finish.

Roses, G. and K.

Start off with a pyramid of sugar. For this your tube requires to be almost upright. Allow to set and then proceed with the outer petals, drawing the tube down in finishing off. For rose making use the curved tubes given above. Keep the bottom of the tube almost touching the centre all the time and the fine point of the tube leaning outwards a little.

Fig. L gives an idea of stalks that can be made quite easy and worked in with the flowers made by No. 2 plain tube.

Piped Flowers and Roses, in Easy Stages.

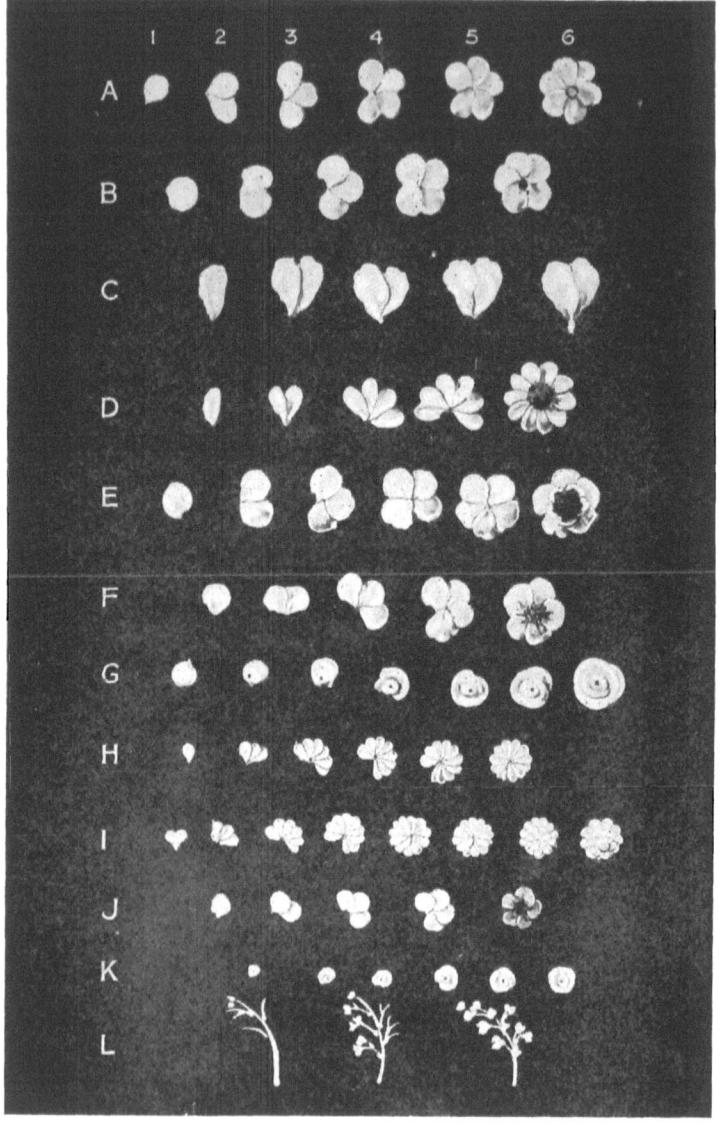

PLATE B.B.

Icing made easy

Cherry Cakes.

3 lbs. 8 ozs. Flour.
2 lbs. 13 ozs. Sugar.
2 lbs. 2 ozs. Butter.
25 Eggs.
2¼ lbs. Cherries cut up with ½ lb. of the flour.
1 lb. Citron (cut up).
Essence of Vanilla.
Method as Bride Cake. Bake in moderate oven.

Madeira Cakes.

4 lbs. Butter.
4½ lbs. Sugar.
4 lbs. Eggs (in shells).
5 lbs. Flour.
¼ lb. Cornflour.
Bare ½ oz. Mixed Powder.
1 Gill Milk.

This mixing turns out a splendid cake and cuts well, and is suitable for pound cakes.

Almond Paste Fruit Cakes.

Mixing Suitable for Large Cakes.

4 lbs. Flour.
4½ lbs. Butter.
4 lbs. Sugar.
4 lbs. Eggs (in shells).
5 lbs. Currants.
2 lbs. Sultanas.
1 lb. Split Almonds.
2 lbs. Cut Mixed Peel.
½ lb. Sliced Citron.
1½ lbs. Cut Cherries.
A little Mixed Spice.
A little Chocolate Colour to darken.

Method as for Bride Cakes. Slow oven. Almond Paste all over after baking. Ruffle a little with a fork, then place in hot oven to colour a little.

Rice Cakes.

1 lb. Butter.
1 lb. 6 ozs. Sugar.
2 lbs. Flour.
1 lb. 4 ozs. Rice (Ground).
¾ oz. Mixed Powder.
1 lb. Cut Lemon Peel.
8 Eggs.
Essence of Lemon.